A Note to Parents

DK READERS is a compelling program for beginning readers, designed in conjunction with leading literacy experts, including Dr. Linda Gambrell, Director of the School of Education at Clemson University. Dr. Gambrell has served on the Board of Directors of the International Reading Association and as President of the National Reading Conference.

Beautiful illustrations and superb full-color photographs combine with engaging, easy-to-read stories to offer a fresh approach to each subject in the series. Each DK READER is guaranteed to capture a child's interest while developing his or her reading skills, general knowledge, and love of reading.

The four levels of DK READERS are aimed at different reading abilities, enabling you to choose the books that are exactly right for your child:

Level 1 – Beginning to read
Level 2 – Beginning to read alone
Level 3 – Reading alone
Level 4 – Proficient readers

The "normal" age at which a child begins to read can be anywhere from three to eight years old, so these levels are only a general guideline.

No matter which level you select, you can be sure that you are helping your child learn to read, then read to learn!

DK

LONDON, NEW YORK, DELHI, PARIS,
MUNICH AND MELBOURNE

Editor Alastair Dougall
Senior Art Editor Nick Avery
US Editor Beth Hester
Production Nicola Torode
Picture Researcher Carolyn Clerkin
Marvel Consultant Seth Lehman

First American Edition, 2003
03 04 05 06 07 10 9 8 7 6 5 4 3 2 1
Published in the United States by DK Publishing, Inc.
375 Hudson Street, New York, New York 10014

Published in Great Britain by Dorling Kindersley Limited.

Library of Congress Cataloging-in-Publication Data
Buckley, James, 1963-
The Incredible Hulk book of strength / written by Jim Buckley.-- 1st
American ed.
p. cm. -- (DK readers, level 4)
Includes index.
Summary: Explores what strength is and how it can be developed using a
comic book character, the Incredible Hulk, to demonstrate, and provides
information on that character and how he came to be.
ISBN 0-7894-9263-6 (pbk. : alk. paper) -- ISBN 0-7894-9543-0 (hc. :
alk. paper)
1. Muscle strength--Juvenile literature. 2. Incredible Hulk
(Fictitious character)--Juvenile literature. [1. Muscle strength. 2.
Strength of materials. 3. Incredible Hulk (Fictitious character)] I.
Title. II. Series: Dorling Kindersley readers. 4. Proficient readers.
QP321.B835 2003
613.7'1--dc21
2002153313

Color reproduction by Media Development and Printing Ltd., England
Printed and bound in China by L Rex Printing Co., Ltd.

The publisher thanks the following for their kind permission
to reproduce their photographs:
c=center; t=top; b=bottom; l=left; r=right

10: Getty Images/Darryl Estrine bl; 16: Corbis/Bettmann tl;
18: Associated Press AP tl; Corbis/Vince Streans bl; 20: Getty Images/Roy Giles
bl; Getty Images News Service/Michael Steele tl; 21: Corbis/Bettmann tr; 22:
Bryan And Cherry Alexander Photography: bl; 23: Corbis/Wally McNamee bl;
Michael S. Yamashita tr; 24: Corbis/Jim Cummins tl; Duomo bl;
25: Corbis/Michael Kevin Daly tr; 26: Corbis tl; 26-27: Getty Images/Jonathan
Scott; 28: Corbis/Kevin Schafer bl; 29: Christian Zuber tr; 32: Corbis/Joe
McDonald bl; 33: Corbis/Amos Nachoun tr; 36: Corbis/Ted Streshinsky tl;
38: Getty Images/Eric Myer tl; 39: Corbis/Christine Osborne tr;
40: Corbis/David Turnley tl; 41: Corbis/Craig Hammell br; 42: Imperial War
Museum tl; 43: Wallace Collection br; 44: Corbis/Lester Lefkowitz tl;
45: Corbis/Bettmann tl; 47: Corbis/Tim Davis tr.

The publishers have tried to trace 29: Christian Zuber tr; without success
and would be grateful if he could contact us so that details can be included in
subsequent reprints.

All other images © Dorling Kindersley.
For further information see: www.dkimages.com

see our complete product line at
www.dk.com

Contents

DK Readers

THE INCREDIBLE
HULK'S™
BOOK OF STRENGTH

Written by Jim Buckley

DK
DK Publishing

The Hulk's softer side
Mild-mannered scientist Bruce Banner turns into the Hulk.

Physicist
This type of scientist studies how matter and energy work together. Often they study radiation (symbol below), which is the energy given off by certain elements.

Who is Hulk?

He's big, he's green, and he's the strongest thing you—or anyone else in the world—has ever seen. The incredible Hulk ripples with muscles, bulges with power, and flexes with so much might that he's a walking powerhouse.

But where did this not-so-jolly green giant come from? What made him so strong? The answer (according to the Marvel Comics writers who created him in 1962) lies in atomic energy.

Marvel told the tale of Dr. Bruce Banner, a very brilliant physicist. Banner had created an extremely powerful gamma bomb.

The first test explosion of the gamma bomb was all set, and a wide area was cleared for safety. Suddenly, a teenager named Rick Jones ran on to the site on a dare.

Banner raced out to save Jones, shoving him to safety just as the gamma bomb blew up! Banner was bathed in eerie, powerful gamma rays. It soon became clear that the rays had transformed Banner. He had changed into the mighty, powerful, incredible Hulk!

Hulk's debut
The first comic book to feature the Hulk was published by Marvel in 1962.

Rippling with muscles, the Hulk combines strength with intense ferocity!

How strong is Hulk?

Since that fateful day of the gamma bomb, Bruce Banner has changed back and forth into the Hulk thousands of times. It is an amazing transformation.

The greatest change to Banner's body—other than his skin turning green!—is the rapid creation of a set of muscles that make him stronger than an entire football team. Hulk stands seven feet (2.13 meters) tall, and weighs 1,040 pounds (468 kilograms), depending on what he had for dinner. He's as tall as the tallest basketball player, but he weighs three times as much!

A less positive change is that his intelligence disappears. While the Hulk is amazingly strong, he often doesn't know how to use his power. "Hulk smash!" is often all he can say as he tears up the landscape.

Ch-ch-changes
Bruce Banner's body isn't the only thing that changes. When he becomes the Hulk, his face becomes a tough-looking mask of power.

Good or bad?
Hulk sometimes doesn't know how to use his strength, and other Marvel heroes, such as Thor, have to step in to help control him.

Hercules
The Greek hero Hercules is another Marvel superhero whose strength is his greatest superpower.

When he doesn't use his strength to break things, Hulk's exploits are breathtaking. He can lift buses full of people, stop trains in their tracks, tear down whole buildings in seconds, or bend thick steel beams like licorice.

Often, Hulk is able to use his strength to help people in trouble, such as Banner's girlfriend Betty Ross or Hulk's friend Rick Jones. Though Hulk seems like a brute, he has a mellow center. Villains make a big mistake when they get him angry.

The powerful arms of the Hulk can tear through thick, iron bars like limp spaghetti.

His anger only increases his strength. Virtually no superhero or super-villain ever invented can defeat the Hulk in one-to-one combat. His fists are like battering rams when he punches and his kick can topple mountains.

Gamma radiation gave the incredible Hulk a kind of strength not seen in any creature in the real world. In this book, we'll compare Hulk's strength to people, machines, animals and more.

Hulk's strength is just one of his many talents. We'll also see that he can leap like a kangaroo on the moon and recover instantly from injury. And though he isn't the smartest giant in the world, he does have unique mental abilities.

Now. . . Hulk read!

The Thing
Though not quite as strong as Hulk, The Thing boasts some of Marvel's mightiest muscles.

Thor is the Thunder God. He wields his magic hammer like Hulk uses his fists.

Measuring weight
There are two types of systems to measure weight. The English system uses pounds; the metric system uses kilograms. One pound (lb) equals .45 kilograms (kg).

The more we use our muscles, the bigger they grow.

Strong muscles

Strength can mean many different things. One dictionary says that strength is "the quality of being strong," which doesn't really answer the question, does it? So look under strong: "capable of exerting great power." That's more like it!

In Hulk's case, he can exert, or use, much more power than the rest of us. But when he calls on this great power, he is using pretty much the same method that human beings use when they need strength. Hulk is using muscles.

Your body's bony skeleton is surrounded by a network of long, ropy strands. These muscle strands work together in groups to make your bones move, whether that means walking or running or lifting or even eating.

Together, your bones and muscles are what give you strength.

Hulk has the same major muscle groups as humans. . . they're just much bigger and much stronger. On this page, we've shown on Hulk what some of the most important muscles are and what they're called.

Short but big
Muscles pull on bones by getting shorter. This makes them bulge a little.

Triceps

Trapezius

Biceps

Flexor

Abdominals

Adductor

Quadriceps

Eat up!
Muscles in the bodies of living things work by turning food energy into motion.

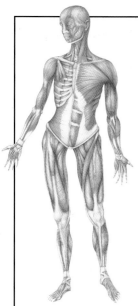

Other muscles
The muscles
we'll talk about
in this book are
called skeletal
muscles. Your
body also has
smooth muscles
which are
found in your
intestines,
among other
places.

*Hulk's no show-
off, but when he
flexes his biceps in
a classic muscle-
man pose, it's
pretty impressive.*

All of the muscles in your body
(and, of course, in Hulk's) work in
pairs. One set of muscles moves a
bone one way; the matching set
moves it the other way. For example,
Hulk's biceps muscle pulls his
forearm up while his triceps muscle
lowers his forearm.

You have muscles in every part
of your body, each moving different
parts of your skeleton when your
brain tells them to move. That's why
they're also called voluntary muscles.

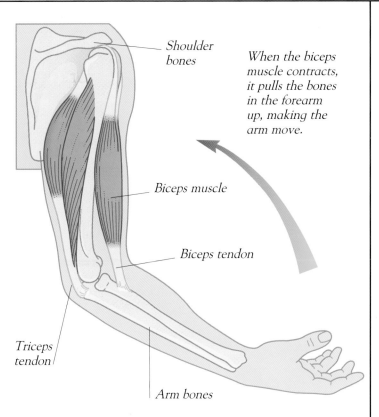

Shoulder bones

When the biceps muscle contracts, it pulls the bones in the forearm up, making the arm move.

Biceps muscle

Biceps tendon

Triceps tendon

Arm bones

Your leg muscles won't make you walk until they get a signal from your brain to get moving.

Muscles in your heart and lungs are called involuntary. You don't have to tell your heart to pump or your lungs to breath. Those muscles do that specialized work on their own (we hope!).

Muscle man
Some muscles join to bones. When we want to move, they pull the bones into position.

The red parts are muscle fibers. The white strands at the end are tendons that attach muscles to bones.

Thump, thump
Your heart is made of a special type of muscle called cardiac muscle.

Your body uses arm muscles and leg muscles to do a sport like this tug-of-war.

13

Tiny muscles
Hulk's powerful muscles are great for tearing down buildings. But he also has enough control of smaller muscles to do more delicate operations.

Contract
A word that means to tighten. Muscles tighten when they do their work.

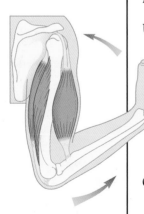

Muscles are made up of individual strands of tissue wound together. They look very much like a rope. This helps make muscles strong, and also very elastic, or stretchy.

When Hulk's brain signals his muscles to move, they perform a unique and powerful trick. They contract. That is, they shrink the bundle of muscles being moved. This brings the two bones closer together, along with any small buildings he is lifting.

This contraction in pairs of muscles is what lets your body (and Hulk's) perform any action that requires strength. That means everything from running to jumping to carrying groceries in from the car.

Muscles also help perform other feats that don't need much strength. When you thread a needle, for instance, your finger muscles must grab the tiny thread and then aim it through the needle's opening. This doesn't take much strength, but it does take muscles!

Now let's look at what the Hulk (and some people) can do with muscles.

Dexterity
This word describes the ability to do small or intricate things with your hands, using your muscles, of course.

Eyes front!
Believe it or not, it takes six individual "extraocular" muscles working together to move one of your eyes in any direction.

While Banner needs glasses to see, the Hulk's eye muscles help give him perfect vision.

Heart work
Any kind of exercise you do is building muscles. The more you work your body, the stronger your heart becomes, and remember: It's a muscle, too!

Weights
Lifting iron weights is one way that people build up their muscles.

Strong people

Hulk has enormous muscles and can do things that normal people can't do. However, Hulk doesn't need to work out at a gym. Thanks to gamma energy, he's a naturally powerful being.

Regular people, though, can build up their muscles to make them bigger and to make their bodies stronger. You've probably seen people lifting weights, running, or working on exercise machines. They are doing this to improve the size and quality of their muscles. Muscles that don't get used can become smaller and softer.

Weightlifting is a good way to develop muscles. Young people should make sure to check with a teacher or coach before trying weight training. You should also always work with a partner when lifting heavy weights.

When using weights or weight machines, you are making your muscles work harder. Working harder makes them stronger, and, in some cases, bigger. Stronger muscles can help your body in many ways, from improving your posture to giving you more energy. You won't be the Hulk, but you'll feel better! With proper supervision, lifting weights can help any person gain strength and power.

Hulk: big.
Banner: small.

Yoga
Exercises like yoga help keep muscles limber and flexible.

Strength in a crisis
Rescue workers need strength when they lift stretchers or carry gear used to help people in trouble.

On the job
Whether carrying wood, loading bricks, or pounding nails, builders need strength.

Beyond helping a person stay healthy, the strength of muscles helps some people use strength every day in their work. Construction workers lift heavy materials, swing hammers, or use saws. Miners dig for minerals using good-old-fashioned shovels, along with high-tech drills. Firefighters have to wear more than 50 pounds (22.5 kg) of gear and carry heavy hoses up ladders.

People who deliver packages or the mail have to use strength to carry their loads. Sometimes even surgeons need strength to perform their jobs, such as when a doctor resets a patient's separated shoulder.

All these people use their muscles to do their work. But whether you know it or not, you also use muscles all the time; you're using muscles right now reading this book. Your eye muscles are moving

Light load
A fairly strong person can lift about 150 pounds (67.5 kg). The Hulk can do a bit better; this army tank sent to capture Hulk by General Ross weighs about 67 tons, but to Hulk it's as light as a feather!

Lots of lifting
The World's Strongest Man competition is held in cities around the world. Mighty competitors lift tires, carry heavy stones for distance, play tug-of-war against cars, and battle through other tests of strength.

to follow the words. Your hand muscles are helping you hold the book. Your fingers turn the pages. You and every other human being (and animal!) use muscles in almost every part of life.

Shot put
In the shot put, athletes use this special method to throw a 16-pound (7.2 kg) iron ball for distance.

Caber tossing
The caber toss is a unique event from Scotland. Strong men try to flip over the wooden caber, which is about as big as a telephone pole.

Strong sports

Athletes need strength to perform every sport from ping-pong to polo. Some sports, however, favor those with great strength.

Weightlifting is not only good exercise, as we saw in the last chapter, it's also a competitive sport. Fortunately for the weightlifters of the world, Hulk is not eligible to enter. He would win hands down—or should we say, hands up?

Weightlifters compete against others of similar weight. That is, a 200-pound (90-kg) man competes against men who are also about 200 pounds. Women, too, have become very active in weightlifting, and both men's and women's events are part of the Summer Olympics.

Weightlifters compete in several events. In the clean-and-jerk they have to lift a weight to their shoulders and then above their heads. In the snatch, they lift the weight from the ground directly over their head. In the press, they raise a weight from a metal frame.

The most weight that any human being has lifted at one time is 6,270 pounds (2,821 kg). Paul Thomas Anderson, a champion American lifter, hoisted that much on his back in 1957.

Mighty Russian
The Hulk-like Vasili Alexeyev of the USSR dominated international weightlifting competitions in the 1970s.

Go ahead, make his day
The Hulk would easily dominate any athletic contest he entered. He not only has enormous strength, but he absolutely refuses to back down or lose. Just ask any villain he's defeated.

Power punch
Hulk takes his cue from boxing when he uses his mighty fists to knock out his opponents.

Ear's looking at you
In the Eskimo Games, you might see this unusual ear-pulling contest. Basically, it's a two-person tug-of-war, but with ears instead of hands.

Another type of sport that demands strength is wrestling. Matched against opponents who are about the same size, wrestlers must use only the strength of their arms, legs, and bodies to defeat their opponents. Hulk often uses wrestling moves when grappling with enemies.

The real incredible hulks of the sports world are the sumo wrestlers from Japan. These guys are so big, they could probably give Hulk a run for his money.

Sumo wrestlers sometimes weight as much as 600 pounds (270 kg) or more! Wearing not much more than a diaper, they face each other in a small ring. The first wrestler to be forced from the ring or to fall to the ground is the loser. Sumo is hugely (pardon the pun!) popular in Japan.

Sumo
In Japan, sumo is as popular as baseball is in America. The man in black is a referee, not a wrestler.

Other sports where strength can play a big part include American football, where linemen can weigh 400 pounds (180 kg), and rugby, in which muscles are the only pads!

On the line
Football players need strength and balance when they clash at the line of scrimmage. Huge linemen bash together at the start of every play, trying to help their team move the ball.

Up and away
In the pole vault, athletes use a flexible pole to help them jump as high as 20 feet (6 meters).

Go long!
After taking a running start, long jumpers can leap nearly 30 feet (9 meters), landing in a sandy pit.

Giant leaps

Try this experiment to test the strength of your legs... well, first read this experiment, put down the book, and then try it.

Stand with your feet as wide as your shoulders. Swing your arms and see how far you can jump— probably about 3 or 4 feet (1 meter). Now look out your window. Find the farthest object you can spot. Believe it or not, Hulk could jump from where you're sitting to that object.

Hulk's super-strong leg muscles give him leaping ability that means he is almost flying. You probably walk to many places, ride your bike, or drive with your parents. Hulk jumps. He can cover thousands of yards with these leaps, taking him great distances in just a short time. If he has to, he can cover enormous distances with these leaps. He once jumped across the Atlantic Ocean!

He can also jump up a long way, too. No need for elevators or even airplanes when you've got legs like Hulk's.

People in sports often use great leaping ability, too. In track and field, there are several jumping events, including the long jump and the high jump. In basketball, players with "great hops" soar toward the hoop like Hulks in shorts.

Hoop hops
The basketball rim is 10 feet (3 meters) high. Players often need to jump while playing.

Look, up in the sky! Is it a giant green meteor? No, it's just the Hulk, who leaps instead of taking long walks.

Strong animals

So far, we've only looked at people and how they use strength to live and work. What about other animals?

Just like human beings, animals turn food energy into motion and power. They use all sorts of special muscles to do this. And for many types of animals, strength means life.

Measuring power
Scientists and engineers measure engines and other power plants using horsepower, which is the energy used to move 1,000 pounds (450 kg) 33 feet (10 meters) in one minute.

Animal hulks
They're not green, but they're bigger than the Hulk. Elephants can weigh more than 12,000 pounds (540 kg). Hulk, however, is stronger than an elephant.

What is the strongest type of animal in the world? Well, you can certainly look at the largest animals first. Elephants can move tremendous weights, and in fact have been trained to carry trees in some countries. Rhinoceroses can go head-to-head with a moving car and come out a winner. (In fact, the Hulk has battled a villain called the Rhino on many occasions.) Polar bears can carry 500-pound (225-kg) walruses on their backs for miles.

Not Yogi
Hulk-sized bears are among the largest and strongest mammals in North America. Male black bears can weigh 700 pounds (315 kg).

What about dinos?
Dinosaurs had to be very strong. The largest had to be strong enough to carry their own weight of more than 55 tons (49,500 kg)!

27

Parking problems?
The Hulk is the only "animal" that could do this to a car!

Mighty insect
Light to you, this leaf is enormous to an ant, yet it can lift it with ease.

However, the best way to judge an animal's strength is to look at its proportional strength. This means comparing what an animal can lift to how much it weighs. A strong person, for instance, can lift about three times his body weight. An elephant can lift about one-quarter of its body weight, but that is still more weight than just about any other animal can lift.

Insects, however, are perhaps the strongest type of animal because they can lift objects that weigh many, many times more than they do. The strongest insect is the rhino beetle, which can lift 850 times its own weight! That would be like a person being able to carry around 40 passenger cars!

Ants can lift huge weights, compared to their size. A twig or leaf might not weigh too much to you (or to the Hulk, of course). To an ant, it's the size of a refrigerator, yet they can pick it up with ease.

For these animals, being this strong is the only way that they can survive.

Gotta hand it to them
Part of the reason that apes and gorillas are stronger is the size of their hands and muscles, here compared to a human's.

Man, monkey, or Hulk?
Being a human being under all that green, Hulk has muscles that are similar to apes and chimps. These animals have muscles and skeletons similar to those of people.

The silverback gorilla can lift four times as much as a human.

Frilled lizard
If threatened, this little lizard flares out a large fan of skin around its neck and suddenly it looks much more fierce!

Painful change
His skin bulges, his muscles enlarge, and his skin turns dark green! Changing into the Hulk is hard on Bruce Banner, but it's even harder on his shirts, which end up in tatters!

Transformations

Along with strength, Hulk shares another unique strength, or ability, with some animals.

When Bruce Banner is threatened or angry, his body transforms into the Hulk.

Some animals have the same power: they change the shape or color of their bodies to defend against attack. Nature has provided this defense mechanism, while gamma radiation did the same for Hulk.

Chameleons are the most well-known animal "transformers." They change the color of their skin to match their surroundings. A green chameleon can appear brown when hiding in a tree, for instance. Green skin doesn't help the Hulk hide, however.

Other animals change to appear more fierce, much as the Hulk looks a bit more menacing than humble Bruce Banner. Dogs, for instance, raise the hair on their backs to appear larger. Cats arch their backs, while owls and other birds spread their wings to scare predators. In the animal kingdom, change is good.

Puffer fish
The humble little puffer fish suddenly becomes a spike-covered ball when it is threatened.

Butterfly
Perhaps the most amazing animal transformation occurs when caterpillars emerge from their cocoons as butterflies and moths!

Powerful antiseptic
Some types of mammals, such as dogs, can help repair cuts or scrapes by licking them. Their saliva contains substances that speed healing.

Tale of a tail
Some types of lizards have an amazing healing ability. If their tail is lost to a predator or in an accident, they can grow a new one!

Healing powers

If you get a cut on your finger, you might put on a bandage and several days later, the cut will have healed. If you sprain your ankle, you put ice on it, and eventually it feels better.

The Hulk, however, often has to deal with injuries much more dangerous and painful than a cut or a sprain. When his body is battered, bruised, and beaten by the super-villains he is constantly at war with, he relies on another of his amazing abilities. The Hulk's gamma-ray-enhanced body can heal itself. Just give the Hulk a few minutes to relax, and his body can make itself whole again.

Some members of the animal kingdom possess a similar healing ability, though they don't heal quite as quickly as the Hulk. Sea stars and lizards can regrow limbs.

Arms or legs?
Sea stars are a type of animal called an echinoderm. If they lose an arm (or is it a leg?), they can regrow it.

However, it can take them many months to complete the regrowth.

Some animals go to considerable lengths to avoid being hurt or getting ill. Monkeys and bears rub themselves with fragrant oils to ward off insect stings. Tortoises walk many miles to find calcium that helps maintain their shells.

In a battle with his enemy Vector, Hulk had all of his skin pulled off his body. Yet in a few moments, his healing ability let him return to normal.

Lots of candles
The oldest human beings ever have lived to be more than 120 years old.

Here today. . .
On the opposite end of the life spectrum is the mayfly. Once they reach the adult stage, they live only a few hours, just long enough to lay their eggs.

Long life

The Hulk has been rampaging through the pages of Marvel Comics since 1962. That means he is more than 40 "years" old. In that time, Bruce Banner might have added some of those years, Hulk reveals another unique ability: Hulk never really ages. Thanks to the gamma radiation that built his big green body, the Hulk is not affected by time like other humans.

As Banner ages, the question will have to be answered: What will happen when Banner becomes very old? Will he ever die? Will he become the Hulk permanently?

Stay tuned to the comic books to find out what happens!

Meanwhile, in the animal kingdom, some species are able to defeat time for a while. Some turtles and whales can live to nearly 100 years old.

Condors and parrots have lived more than 50 years. Human beings can live to be more than 100; our average lifespan is 75 years. Elephants are the longest-living, non-human land mammal, hanging in there until they're more than 40.

Giant tortoise
The box turtle is the longest-living animal, often reaching more than 100 years of age. Compare that to the average dog or cat, who might only live as long as 12-20 years.

Not even the calendar can stop the mighty Hulk. Like that bunny in the battery commercial, he just keeps going and going and going…

Machine power

So far, we've looked at how living things use strength and other powers that the Hulk possesses.

Machines also use strength, though of course they don't have muscles. Also, instead of food energy, they use various kinds of fuel to drive their engines and parts.

Hulk has gone up against machines, from giant locomotives to fabulous creations sent to Earth by aliens. And he has smashed them all! However, in most cases, machines are much stronger than humans.

Chop it up!
A jackhammer is a powerful machine tool used to break through hard concrete or asphalt.

Lifting power
This enormous truck crane needs cables, hooks, gears, and a mighty motor to do what Hulk can do with his bare hands.

C 500

Pile driver
A machine called a pile driver uses a large block to smash holes. Hulk, of course, needs only his fist to break through thick walls like tissue paper.

Machines are built to do things for us that Hulk can do with ease. They use various kinds of mechanisms, controlled by drivers or machine operators. Different machines lift heavy objects, transport massive weights, smash enormous rocks, or dig huge holes.

The K-1000 tower crane, for instance, can lift more than 130 tons (117,000 kg). Imagine moving 20 elephants in the length of a football field.

Digging deep
An earth-moving machine in Pennsylvania called Big Muskie has a scoop so big, an entire marching band can fit inside. Big Muskie can move 19.5 tons (17 million kg) in an hour!

Under pressure
The tires on these enormous dump trucks are more than 10 feet tall!

Heavy load
Wheel loaders can fill their front shovels with tons of rocks and dirt.

Let's look at the biggest machines on wheels. A dump truck used in mining operations is more than 60 feet tall (18 meters)! The Terex Titan 33-19 has wheels taller than any man, and it can hold more than 350 tons (315,000 kg) of dirt and rock. That means it can carry the weight of three blue whales!

Giant dump trucks like this one combine size with strength. Their heavy metal bodies support the huge weight, much as the Hulk's giant frame does.

Other giant trucks haul freight or work underground in other mines. Giant tunnel-digging machines plow through the earth like enormous moles. In Australia, huge trucks with a dozen trailers haul entire herds of cows across the Outback.

Whether they are used to carry huge loads, lift giant objects, or move earth, machines are one way to get a little bit of Hulk in our day.

Smoothing the way
Powerful bulldozers use wide metal blades to move huge amounts of earth, sand, or gravel.

Like a walking bulldozer, Hulk can rip up pavement like paper.

Bashing ball
Cranes swing a huge iron ball to knock down buildings.

Demolition man

People use machines and powerful explosives to do what the Hulk can do with his bare hands: demolish buildings.

When a building is old, damaged, or in the way of another project, it is destroyed by collapsing it. Explosives are often used, along with heavy equipment. The buildings fall to the earth in a mighty cloud of dust.

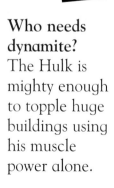

Who needs dynamite?
The Hulk is mighty enough to topple huge buildings using his muscle power alone.

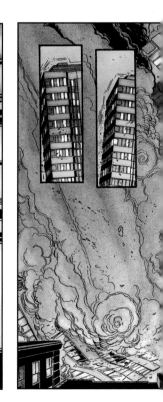

12 MAIN

THOOOM

These displays of man's might often make for spectacular pictures. Crowds of people gather to watch these shows of destruction.

Hulk doesn't want a crowd to gather when he has to knock down a building. He is rarely as careful as demolition experts. In fact, sometimes he is trying to knock a structure *onto* his enemy.

When Hulk and Juggernaut battled on an army base, they tossed whole buildings at each other. In the end, only the Hulk was left standing amid the debris.

Big whap!
Slamming his enormous hands together creates a shock wave that can knock over the most powerful opponents without the Hulk needing to touch them.

Going down
Demolition experts use explosives to carefully bring down unused, older buildings.

Tough skin

The Hulk's enemies, including villains like The Leader and Modok, have spent years aiming weapons at his green skin. Even the U.S. Army has fired thousands of bullets, missiles, laser beams, and bombs at Hulk. But nothing has ever stopped him, thanks to his invulnerable skin.

Hulk's skin has been green or gray throughout his life (though oddly, his pants are nearly always purple or blue). But it's not the unusual color that makes his thick skin able to resist projectiles of all types. The gamma radiation transforms his skin into iron!

Body armor
Military and police forces often wear clothing made of materials such as Kevlar, super-thick plastic that can stop bullets.

Steel on wheels
Heavy steel military vehicles roll into battle on rubber and metal treads.

Armor on tanks can be several inches thick.

Throughout history, people have used many different methods to try to have protection like the Hulk's. Early Roman armies wore metal helmets, chest guards, and shin plates. Knights in the Middle Ages wore entire suits of armor. Their horses wore armor too.

Modern soldiers wear thick helmets and different types of body armor made of space-age plastic. They also use heavy vehicles, from tanks to armored cars, that can withstand powerful blasts.

The Hulk can use his massive, bulletproof body as a shield to protect nonbulletproof human beings from harm.

Dragon protection Medieval knights used steel armor such as this breastplate.

Cat sense
Some animals seem to have senses beyond sight, sound, and the rest. This "sixth sense" lets them sense danger or sudden changes in the weather.

The mind of the Hulk

Strength in muscles and body. . . strength in engines and machines . . . what about strength of mind?

Bruce Banner is gifted with one of the greatest minds on the planet. He understands the amazing physical forces that form the world. When he turns into the Hulk, however, he forgets most of that wonderful knowledge.

But as the Hulk, he has gifts that he does not have when he is Bruce Banner. Along with rippling muscles, the Hulk has an amazing ability that is somewhat like extrasensory perception, also called ESP.

ESP means the ability to see things that are far away from you, out of sight of your eyes, or the ability to "sense" things that might happen in the future. For instance, a person with this gift might be able to sense the arrival of a visitor long before that person has arrived.

In recent stories, fans of the Hulk have learned that part of the reason that Banner becomes the Hulk is in response to trauma suffered as a child. When he turns into the Hulk, his fear of this trouble returning allows his mind to be aware of things his eyes can't see.

I see you! Ghosts may or may not be real, but they pop up in Hulk's world once in a while. Invisible to most beings, they are visible to the Hulk.

Hulk's mind power does not equal his muscle power, but his brain does give him some special gifts.

Going home

Another of the Hulk's gamma-given mental gifts is a remarkable homing instinct. This usually means the ability to return to the place one was born; in the Hulk's case, that is the desert plain where he was bathed with rays from the gamma bomb.

No matter where he is, he can return to that spot without a map, without a vehicle.

Some animals also have a similar ability to find their way home. Salmon are one of the most amazing examples of this uncanny ability.

Long flights
Monarch butterflies fly thousands of miles to return to the exact trees where they were born in order to lay their eggs.

When it is time for salmon to lay eggs, they return to the ponds where they were born. But often this means swimming *up* a raging river! They fling themselves up waterfalls, leap through raging rapids. They are driven by a mysterious inner force that they must obey.

In times of stress, Hulk relies on this ability, too, and returns to the place he calls home.

The Hulk brings a lot of power to the table when battling the forces of evil. He boasts invulnerable skin, incredible leaping ability, and unique mental powers. But those abilities all are secondary to his strength. Hulk is simply the strongest two-legged being in the world. If you want to argue with him about that, be our guest!

Sniff, sniff
Using smell and other senses, dogs and cats can often find their way homes from great distances.

Feathered telegraph
Pigeons can be trained to fly back and forth from specific points, racing or carrying messages.

Glossary

biceps
The muscle at the front of a person's arm. When contracted, it raises the forearm.

bunker
An underground room or building, often used to protect the occupants from explosions.

cardiac muscles
Special muscles that form a person's heart.

contraction
The act of making something smaller, in this case, a muscle or muscle group.

debris
The remains of something that has been destroyed or knocked down.

demolish
Completely destroy, usually by a very large force of some kind.

echinoderm
A type of animal without a bony skeleton that is usually shaped in a circular pattern. Examples include sea stars and sea urchins.

elastic
Able to be stretched.

enhanced
Improved; made better.

ESP
Short for extrasensory perception; the ability to see things that are not there, to predict the future, or to see things out of one's own sight.

exert
To put forth or to put into use, usually into action.

extraocular
The name for muscles that surround and move a person's eyes.

gamma bomb
A fictional type of explosive invented in 1962 by Dr. Bruce Banner. When it exploded and he was caught in its radiation blast, he was turned into the Hulk.

grappling
Fighting, wrestling.

involuntary
Not of one's own choice.

invulnerable
Unable to be harmed in any way.

medieval
Referring to the period of history from about 500 to 1500 A.D.

physicist
Scientist who studies how matter and energy work together.

projectiles
Objects that are shot or thrown through the air.

proportional
Corresponding in size or intensity to something else.

radiation
Energy sent out (emitted) by various elements or minerals.

skeletal muscles
Muscles in the human body that are attached to the skeleton and are used to move bones.

skeleton
The bones of an animal's body.

sumo
A type of wrestling popular in Japan, performed by enormous athletes in a small ring.

transformation
A change, usually massive and dramatic.

trauma
Especially painful physical or mental injury.

voluntary
Of one's own choosing.